FROM *B*EYOND THE *G*RAVE

MANOJ BHAGWANDIN

From Beyond the Grave

Copyright © 2025 by Manoj Bhagwandin.

MILTON & HUGO L.L.C.
4407 Park Ave., Suite 5
Union City, NJ 07087, USA

Website: *www. miltonandhugo.com*
Hotline: *1- 888-778-0033*
Email: *info@miltonandhugo.com*

Ordering Information:
Quantity sales. Special discounts are granted to corporations, associations, and other organizations. For more information on these discounts, please reach out to the publisher using the contact information provided above.

Library of Congress Control Number: IN-PROCESS
ISBN-13:   979-8-89285-739-0   [Paperback Edition]
                  979-8-89285-740-6   [Digital Edition]

Rev. date: 11/17/2025

-Words from the other side. Other side of emotions and a life no longer that weighs one down.

FEATHERS

My back is pulsating with thorns
My feet as light as the wind that drifts me to places unknown
My hands together with my very breath gasping for the world
The world to see the reflection of a white cloud over blue skies
in a summers evening
My feathers they carry me, but also the weight of agony's warm
embrace

THEATER FACES

Am I supposed to be me in this world
The me that dances to tunes not yet heard
The me that talks sweet roses into the air that feels like thorns
when taking a breathe
The me that walks with their head up like clouds guide their
every step
or the me that painted its face the masses assumed me to be

RED

A glimpse of gasping breaths I met,
With tears of burgundy silhouettes
I wipe the paint from my eyes
And dash it on the canvas I once called
My heart is full and null in scripture
You've been the only figure
I can remember

ECLIPSE

You've caused an eclipse my heart can't hold.

Shade the sun, and what was warm

Turns colder than I thought possible.

Vessels freeze, as if you stilled time.

Caught in breaths I fought to keep,

My eyes see only the glory you cast upon me

GLIMMER

Looking to the skies with glimmer in my eyes
You shine through my heart where the wind is crisp
A breath of fresh air as reviving as a smile from your lips
Tears they fall but they blossom petals through the cracks on
the floor
Because my spirits been graced
By a love that waters my broken soul

SERENE

Seen by the eyes of many
Understood by few
The wind it sings a song of your name
Words understood too softly
Presence felt loudly
Reflections on my past
I wish you very pleasant futures
Ever so serene
I call on your name

MOUNTAINS

Quite mind with mountains of thoughts
Loud feelings with regret in my heart
For the person I should've been
Roses burning with ashes of gold dust
This life I'm in
Darkness engulfs the soul
Vibrancy glimmer in the wounds
Take my heart and make it bleed
My life is lost, waiting for the one I need
Take my sorrow and bury it with a smile
Pint of tears that follows my happy cries
For I mourned a life that hasn't begun
A life to live with fragrance of your love

LINGERING SHADOWS

The shadows whisper secrets,
A darkness stirs within,
Beware the secrets of the past,
The night holds a thousand fears,
The veil between worlds is thin,
A chilling presence lingers,
Where the moon casts no light, and
The heart knows what the mind cannot see

A DEEP REMEMBRANCE

Forgetting who I was I became everyone
I never felt right to me
So I became who I thought I would like myself to be
Until I realized I never liked that idea of me
Until i closed my eyes and opened them knowing it's who I came
here to be
Secured and knowing no one can ever be me

A WALK

The trees they say closer
The wind hums a lullaby
Birds they leave a trail of feathers
Across the sky the portraits remind me of a place I see in
dreams
When the breath for air begins, the chaos in my mind meets
its end

TRAIL

Snow to the left
Rain to the right
Weight on me
Sand below
With the sorrows behind me
The pain is ever yearning
Only I know the path I'll go
To follow a trail that leads to summers road

PEN TO PAPER

Art in its many forms
Compare not to elegant words placed on the sky of white
Deep is only the meaning as it comes from the heart
Cast your light and put your heaviness down
The eyes meet each syllable with your own magnificent touch

THESE PALMS

Writing on paper with the tears that drown it
Ever crinkly they speak of lightning and thunder behind it
I clasp my palms together they will never be lonely
As the whispers from my heart fill the room from darkness to
embers

I SEE DEAD PEOPLE

The faces I see are of the ocean of blood, life, and agony
They walk this Earth of ego and a tale of the dying sun
Fear me not they say, as the open their tongues
Only they will walk this plane of misery until they cry
They bottle and suppress the very living,
Very soulful and vibrant life they wish they already have

DANCING

An innocent soul with sinner tendencies
Walking the road lonely the minds filled with bad company
I know it's not right but it feels so good to me
I know the devils tricks, he tries my sanity
If I had to fight the devil I have to make him understand me
See i didn't fight a fair match
It might've been fixed for me
Just know he didn't have the spirit like me

PRIDE

As sturdy as an anchor in the tides
A proud man once sat and his mind ever so stiff
He lived a life of regret and grit
Losing love, lost him his soul
That one lonely night
Forever he was, standing high as his might
Until he was saved
By the one who we call many names

RESTING

Is it peace that chooses me?
Or the thought of it to be?
At peace I stand but when I lay rest takes over me
Will the calm ever soothe the ache in my fortress?
Will the trees shake in reverence in the storms its yet to see?

LOST AT SEA

I hear your ships are coming in
Does your cargo bargain for feelings you've yet witnessed
or do they sell for prices the rich may never reach?
Let them come
Let them sail
Only more ships are to come if you know how to tell a tale

DECAY

I buried a blue flower today
It was surrounded by friends but of a different spectrum
They wept of colors of shadow
Almost mourning as if it were dead
Not knowing that the blue was meant to share a light
In their emotions of despair

PEEKING THROUGH THE TREES

I see the Sun through the leaves
I think it speaks to me
Staring through the glimmer
The branches surround
My mind in a cocoon
Not moving a muscle

PASSING

I wish I hung around long enough
Enough to see you belong with me
As far as the eye can see
You haven't meant much to me
For this bond is the only thing left between you and me

APATHY

Apathetic my feelings don't feel
Searching for a feeling
To give my life meaning
I see my head churning

UNWORTHY

The curtains close
I feel unworthy
They world they had stopped to stare
But now they aren't there
Who knew
That i had a moment there
Who knew
I've been followed here

THE ALCHEMIST

You don't have to go there
For I went for you
With a torch that bleeds fire
With a torch that sings too
With a torch that carries grief
And turns it to fireflies
They walk this path besides me
Paying homage to your name too

PAINT MY FLAWS

Brush the strokes in an unequal manner
Parallel the lies and grieving
Contrast the sorrow with blood
Tint the shadows with the heart
You've ripped out of my treasure chest
Pause for a revelation
To the masterpiece you've created

INSECURE

I look at you with hollowed eyes
Silver running down one
Gold from the other
Blood from the one above
Something turns in me
No longer a faint death but a grand awakening
To the possibility
I can be more than I'm meant to be

RAINBOW

A rainbow is a array of emotions
It's also the moment we experience it
It may last forever if you let it
Let it glimmer your eyes
Break your smile and
Cost you your life
For this rainbow isn't just worthwhile
It's the very thing that makes you you

ALCHEMY

I wrote a name down that turned to a blue flame
I described it to a point that sits on a mountain top
Until it turned purple
Down came the mountain
I'm left with a yellow smile

DEPTHS

Valleys that whisper sweet endings
Heaviness that creeps with no warning
Deep down under an underworld
I consider my home
To keep me grounded when the world
Becomes numb

IN LOVE

In love with the shadows I seek to find them
In everyone
Befriending them before the first hello
They don't see the real me
Under a glimmering haze of rainbows

MOONLIGHT

The clouds drift apart only to come together
Blocking my gaze of moonlight
I've hoped to enter
Of a night so gloomy
Without my lover
The clouds remind me
Only those that let go can truly see

GREY

The clouds they say come this way my dear
Come flow with me don't despair
The Sun will guide you and I will hide you
Help protect that light which dwells inside you

CRACK

Broke, I'm broken
The pieces they no longer carry shapes but fragments
Of a light I once had
Fearing placing them back together will hold a new story
One that doesn't pay respect to the past I once had
Kintsugi holds no place in my heart,
for the colors I bear will shatter it again.

ADDICT

My love for a muse
My love to feel something new
Who'd knew I'd make this addiction my master
This pain I sit with festers
Hoping another day I take this crutch and have it lifted
This ray of hope I've been gifted

CRESCENT

The moon isn't crescent anymore
So is my heart
I feel the full force of waves that wait to tear it apart
Cast a blue-hued shadow upon the one I call from the gallows
The mist I mistook for my undying love

HAUNTED

The moon isn't even full yet
I feel the motions you've helped burst open my bleeding heart
Flowers dripping from my hands as I place it back together
This cold chamber which I've yet opened once again
Is met with a glistening apparition with a dress
As white met with hues of vignette

SUN GAZING

Lift my head
Let my eyes be met
With a glance that stills time and
Of light that takes my very breathe

TAKE ME

I can't give you the world
But take parts of me
That the world has left its imprint on
For they'll show you what carved me
They'll hold you as they neglected me
Be sure of you as they forgot me

DAZED AND CONFUSED

Lost in the path I think there's nowhere to go
I look for a sign to bring me back home
I've been lost for some time now
I guess when the path is your mind and destination a smile—
you lose track of time
I close my eyes and clasp my hands and suddenly it's clear
My minds been wandering and a glimpse of happiness appears
I whisper to myself and I can finally hear

HAVING

Having hope is no easy task
It's what you do when you know nothing else
In this world there's a whole to lose it for
But don't make it your last

ZYGOMATICUS MAJOR

Trying to put on a smile for the world
I save myself some tears for later
Laughing I pour it out in my alone time
Captivated by the awe I'm left in
As I pick myself back up only to find
The pieces no longer fit together
So I mold myself anew with stardust to fill its cracks

VILLAIN

This mask I wear is the same one I've used to make peace with
The thoughts I've carried all my life
The racing, the steady, and the sudden
I'll tear it off once I've heard the sweet song
Whispered from your mouth
"With you I am safe here"

KISS OF DEATH

To have been kissed is the blessing
To be touched by it is the curse
I wait for eternity
For a breathe

HUE

Were from the shadows
Of course we know all the tints of black, gray, and blue
But who knows our true colors
The ones you only see with the ones cast from hue

HYMNS FOR THE NIGHT

Walking in the moonlight
Tears hitting my umbrella
I stop to listen to the music
For the genre is not of my choosing
Gaffling howls I hear the shatter
No lightening, no clap no thunder

NOSFERATU

This wine has been too good to me
Your blood would have been too poisonous
The moon no longer lingers in the air
The taste for life no longer sips the same
For eternity I want to rest
Away from you

NECTAR

Life gives its sweetest energy to those who still want a taste
After the insides have been carved and bruised of every
Empathy and bones it once's harnessed
Of every fragility and blood
That once ran its course through its veins
Now stands sweet honey
That's bittersweet

PULVIS ET UMBRA SUMUS

Dust off the gray from the hardened bones
Brush off the webs from the cloth
The seasons they whisper
Delight and solace
To a night that's once old and dark
Peel each eyelid with hands of warm fury
The embracing waits for no one

TWO DOVES

As the boy picked the petals off a lotus
Leaving a warm river of pink to the serene dawn sky
A dove approached in search for a glimpse of remembrance
Of a warmth they once shared
Another dove approaches
On a lotus of white
Bearing gifts for one another
The boy vowed to never pick the lotus apart
As the two doves vowed they'll never part

ANDROMEDA

Oh how the stars will be jealous
Of the galaxy I would paint for you
Every star having a partner
Every planet having a moon
Every comet to visit a friend
And the gravity to bear the name you carry
In every universe you've graced

CANVAS

Rough but still
Frantic but steady
Anxious thoughts paint a pattern of endless streams
Calm ones seem flowing in an essence of grandeur
The centerpiece captures an empty scene

MANE

Dashing white and gold crystalline fortress
At a glance a calm juncture proceeds with innocence
Resting in a jungle of acts and quietness
The lion bows his head down
Resting his mane on the paws of defiance

CROWS

Remind me of my time to come
Announce my arrival
Purple silks embrace
The shadows envelope me in a nights grace

WAIT FOR YOU

I'll stop the very time beneath your feet
Dimensions and galaxies I will cross
To meet you as the first beat the cosmos ever created
The first breath the cosmos ever shared
Engulf me in your eyes and
Witness the creation of a lifelong dream
I'm forever lost in

PATH I WALK

Quite mind with mountains of thoughts
Loud feelings with regret in my heart For the person I should've
been
Roses burning with ashes of gold dust
This life I'm in
Darkness engulfs the soul
Vibrancy glimmer in the wounds
Take my heart and make it bleed
My life is lost, waiting for the one I need
Take my sorrow and bury it with a smile
Pint of tears that follows my happy cries
For I mourned a life that hasn't begun
A life to live with fragrance of your love

SOULMATE

Is it a grievance I don't get to love you
Is it a crime I don't get to make myself whole
Is it true you'd rather not know I exist
Or will the thought of me make you think maybe just maybe
I'm the the one who won

SOUL SONG

Why does my soul feel tormented
Why does living feel cursed
Why does everyone not see me
And why does everyone see me
For who I'm not
Plans fail
Winds gust
My eyes, weary
But my hope
Not lost

CHESS

Why is it when rain pours we shelter away
Like missing our blessings instead of basking in it
Why is it when all hopes lost we never clasp our palms together
Like praying is something foreign, distances away
Why is it when I think of you we get pulled apart
Like the universe's sick game

KUNDALINI

Coiled until the rise
Rise of the serpent
Rise of the phoenix
Rise of the Temple
Transformation
Tell me it's all okay
I know I won't heal linear
But this isn't a race
Time seems still
Yet so fleeting
Don't go back down
To the Sea in which I drowned

BUTTERFLY

This white butterfly
Follows me
Do I leave an essence behind
That lingers in the depths of souls
That yearns for grace
Elegant and transforming
This white butterfly
Leaves me, along with a gentle breeze

WHAT MAKES ME

You are my heartbeat
You are my void
You are my lifeline
My dear,
You know not the impact you
Mean to me
For this love,
Is what makes me

ACT 1

On a stage confessing my love for you
I'm not met with red flowers
Or joyful tears
But memoirs of sorrows
Of things I've yet said

OH MA

Simple yet,
Bold and Majestic yet,
Calmly taken over
By a presence
Graceful yet,
Shaken

RAZOR

Does it sting
Does it ache still Or does it feel like
You're able to breathe
Able to reach again
Feel again
The tears never wounded you
It cleansed you from inside out

COME HOME

How do I take it away?
The sorrow in your heart
The dull ache
The yearning
That feels like strings of yarn wanting to uncoil
The burning to the throat with shoulder blades included
With thoughts of days to come, not even being existent
Tell me
How do I free you
Of this love you've claimed
to say has left you

CLEAR

Smoke running from my eyes
Traces of life hauntingly passing me by
The presence of absence
Without you is clear
Clear I can't function right
When things I planned get left
In the wind
Things such as feelings I will feel
When the rain clears away
But now I see is yet to fade

MEDUSA

I'll let the tears pour down my face
Through every crater and crack and wrinkle
Touch my lips to lift them to a smile
And wipe them away not with a tissue but the very same hands,
That'll heal the world after my eyes have turned it all to stone

WORDS OF TRUTH

Words with a sword
You carry the flame of this mighty torch
As you'll burn yourself sometimes.
As you'll cut through your old self sometimes.
It's still you
Dare to meet yourself for the duel

OUROBOROS

The redundancy of my shortcomings gnaws at my heart
The way in which I wait for a moment of grace for my future to
unfold
Swallows me inside, whole
The cycle ends here I demand
"Wait and see the magnificence" it whispers back

RA

Let no harm enter my dwelling
No malicious face judge the truth which I walk
No energetic leech pull upon my strongholds
See that I am never at fault

THREE WISE MEN

See that the truth is spoken clearly, entering the tombs of men's
ears
Speak the words of mystics as children learning to play
Hear the solace of a kind heart and warn it not to make the
same mistakes

PA

I sometimes ponder the spaces between your eyes
To see me in such a light that fuels me inside
Strength to bear the world and all the thoughts that live in your
mind
Growing old you've been my mirror
Of a man I wish to be by the end of December

BREEZE

Crisp and harsh, the winter's breeze is unbelievably settling
This dusky weather reminds me of a place I once entered
A wonderland filled with adventure, cold and brute with pain as
I ventured
To a place so ghastly not even shadows chose to enter

CIRCLES

You tell me that I've grown
I haven't seen that many lies in all my days here
I still aim to be the little youngster
Who sees fantasy and one love

PROMISES

Whispering hymns in the daytime as one wakes from slumber
Shouting it at night before entering the trance so deep
Promises we keep our mind occupied
With fleeting thoughts so far from reach
Let your chords sing an anthem
In which brings you home

MELANCHOLY

Melancholy rip tides
The shore seems far from the waters
That my soul cries
From the depths of the strings of my heart

INERTIA

What a fool I've been
To let it slip away
The thought of thinking
You away

SWAY ME

Sway with the waters and sit with the moon
A great adventure awaits with me and you
The aurora of the night i'm drunk in love
With the fragment of myself who caught me at first sight

DRUNKEN POETRY

Another glass of your temptation conversations
One more blow of your sweet splendor
My vision is slow and resistant
To looking at your heart that pours
Just one more glass

GLORY BE

Glory be
Finally sound the missing piece
A heart as sweet to set my mind at ease
A smile to make the trees shiver
And my soul to speak
Glory be
I no longer wait or weep
Prayers answered my bones are weak
Clasp my hands I do indeed
My lover has come to me

PAIN

I don't want to leave this world in pain
I want to leave it whole instead of the pieces it's left me in
I'd hold it in my palms as a orb of fragments
Add a touch blood
Pint of sweat
And an ounce of tears

LIFE

Chasing a dream it doesn't let me rest
From the dreary things my heart can't cope
I want to stay in a place that feels like hope
Build a real world that feels magical
More like a fantasy I have no access to

SOMETHING

Something in my head I can't get it out
Something weighing on my mind and can't let it out
Something thoughts put me in doubt
Something happens in my brain I know knotting about

FOR IN LOVE THE SONG NEVER ENDS

The melodies of your voice ring in my ears
The chords you struck haven't left a single tear
In my grand musical I call our undying song
The band of instruments I'll sing all eternity on

CRATERS ON MY SHOULDER

Ill carry the moon to you
When the nights coming in and the colors begin to fade
I'll carry the moon to you
Because you shine bright
I'll carry the moon to you
So the reflection can bring a new color into the sky

ROAR

I want a love that roars like thunder
I want it to cast my down to the arms of my lover
Pleading and counting to see the lightening again
I ask strike me once
So it can take my pain

RUIN

No paper is ruined by thoughts
Paper is only ruined by dreams that never see its reality
Manifest a moment of change
The universe will give you the pen

SENSUAL

Soft and sensual
Caress my shadows
Whisper to my despair
Hold my sorrows
Grieve my tears
Because it won't matter
When you're near

PROFILE

My eyes cried a portrait
My mouth smiled a poem
But my nose
Can't rid the smell of your fragrance
That haunts me

GUST

Your smile takes me where the wind blows
Your cries takes me where the rain pours
But your mind is where I feel home

FIND ME

The peace is still
The stillness is rampant
In my regrets of a future
I've yet met

UNALOME

Life is never a straight line until
The chaos is harnessed
Circles that spiral like a mind
Intertwined in a path of light and dark

PASSERBY

You don't know I exist
Maybe our energies brushed but we are two flames on opposite
beaches
Hopefully looking at the same horizon
You don't know me
But I weave you into my bones
You don't owe me
But I hope I can repay the debt you've left of your presence

EGO

I feel the presence of a monster
The eyes of a beast
Who doesn't gnaw for flesh and bones
But a warm embrace of recognition
It ask gently to see it
And it will loosen its grip

LIFETIME

They say you live only once
But how is it that I die every night?
Has the past I've been living a lie
Or is it the very thing keeping me alive

WHY

Why at death
We hear tales of undying love
For in a day's wake
Our ears grow weary

LIGHTHOUSE

I feel as a pretender to live in this world
To put on a facade of delusions of grandeur
Knowing my heart runs deep as the roots of trees
Crushing me until I'm still
This world I pretend to be in leaves me distilled

GOODBYES

Bury me with a smile
For only a lesson in the path I was
But far greater you were to me
So I ask for my sanity
Bury me with a smile
Because you'd never know the effect you've had on me

TRAGEDY

Oh how've my virtues been written
In a stone that waits to be deciphered
By the next generation of loners
Who wish to feel the Earth's thunder

RACE

I want to race my heart for it beats faster out of my chest
As I gaze upon the river of your ruthless elegance you are
I wish to leap as high as the birds
With how my feelings fly away and wish they were in your arms

MARTYR

You don't have to ask me even once
For the price to pay is little and finite
In a world that shares my love
True love shall reign supreme
As my final wish

WARS

Your eyes paint a picture much more vivid
Your smile wages a war within my mind
For I would fight battles for your heart
Winning every one of them
Losing only when I think of you

ROSES

Red roses falling from the air
A great quarrel upon my ears
Of whom loves whom the most
Arguing, my heart and my mind

GLASS

My eyes are mere glass objects
Made to see reflections I see none other than yours
A reflection that captures the moonlight with none in it
A reflection that shines bright with no Sun
A reflection I've come to love
Because when I look in your eyes
I see stars and the one

A GAZE

Time never stopped so easily
Eyes dancing so elegantly
A dance that feels like eternity
My God so heavenly

ABLAZE

Set my sanity ablaze
This passion with no rage
I come to no senses when I catch a scent
Of the fragrance of life you've left

PSYCH WARD

The halls of my mind are empty
Yet every record of thought turned beautiful memories
I wish to burn it to the ground
In a moment of silence for my nuances
In a final act of glory for my soul

HELLO

I'm afraid of new connections
Because I know the value of grief
What i'm not scared of is saying I love you
Until the very blood in my lungs grow blue

SUFFOCATION

I wrap this iridescent cloak around me—
a fragile shield of shimmer and silence.
It lights the darkness
that strays from the path,
and in its glow,
I create my own.

CIRCLES

My mind does not wander paths—
it spins in circles.
Each step climbs higher,
yet the feeling sinks deeper.
Longing shortens,
while grief becomes unmistakable.
My journey isn't paved in gold—
it's the mud I keep pulling myself from.

ELAPSE

They say time heals,
but time never waited—
not for me to tie my shoes,
nor press my garments.
The wound glows still,
rich with grief, despair, and fear.
And over it all,
hope is the bandage
barely holding on.

A SEED

A seed—
sprouting on a fresh summer's eve.
Winter's longing and despair
left the soul of my body in drought.

I remember:
what has will,
will come my way.

And when I look to the seasons ahead,
a refreshing, thirst-quenching day—
my mind is ready,
my heart steady,
and my soul
will finally take root again.

RING ME DRY

Disappoint me no longer
The stage was only temporary
The heart was only a tool
For what I see now is a weapon
I'll use to finally bash my way through -
The very walls in which you hide behind
Love my dear, ring me dry

SONGS IN WHISPER

Do the dead play symphonies?
Do they miss the waves—
those songs once sung in a warm place?
Do they mourn the ache,
or does it carry them
to their final resting grace?

WAKE ME

Wake me—
Ego, pride, vanity—
when will I escape
the lessons born in a fragile world?

Fear me not,
for love encompasses every part of me.
Does it the same for you?
Of course not—
you've never been held,
never caressed by the light
that radiates the soul you've kept away
in the night's war.

Fight me not—
just dissolve me.

DID I WAKE UP IN A DREAM AGAIN

did i wake up in a dream again,
or was death only a burden
to my wakeful hours?

the agony still protrudes,
the reverence still hums—
a choir rehearsing sorrow,
an orchestra of cruel and brute.

this touching piece of poetry—
i knew it once,
before the silence took its bow.

HUNGER FOR GOLD

pinching for silver and green dust paper
was all i've known.

wishing for gold
in a warm blanket,
the belly hungers
for a taste of salvation.

the mind wanders
through damnation—
a reality i've grown in,
where even the stars
seem fed
from silver platters
and golden spoons.

CROOKED HALO

a trophy upon my head,
celestial—
humming the name of reign.

place it upon every waking soul,
and those who walk with us
no longer.

touch the crowning light.
fix it half-tilted, bright—
one side up
for the path we swore to follow,
one side down
for shadows,
and the things we overcame
with sight.

THE NIGHT, THE MOURNING

Portals burst—
static with a breath lost.

Gasp.
I'm gasping for a second more,
hoping for an eternity less.

Darkness—
pitch black.
Rescue me, light.

The darkness is lifting me
to You—
to finally meet You.

CLOSING PRAYER — THE BECOMING

If you've made it this far,
know you've only just begun the becoming—
as you always have.

Look to the stars
and remember: they are you.
Look into the dark
and know it's you
who's been navigating the light
in your own sacred way.

Breathe fire.
Smile light.
See radiance.
Hear the silence.

The dark was never your enemy—
it was your mirror.
Every tear was a seed,
every ache, a root.
What you called death
was the soul taking off its shoes.

Peace and Love.
Om Shanti.

— Manoj Bhagwandin

I Love You

www.ingramcontent.com/pod-product-compliance
Lightning Source LLC
Chambersburg PA
CBHW051835040426
42447CB00006B/548